"30 Days to Spiritual Enrichment"

Life-Changing
Poetry, Scripture, and Thoughts

By

Barbara A. Caldwell

ISBN: 0-7596-9621-7

This book is printed on acid free paper.

Scripture taken from the Holy Bible: King James Version

1stBooks - rev. 06/11/02

Acknowledgements

I thank my Mother, Hattie Caldwell, my Father, Quitman Caldwell, and all others, who prayed for me and believed in me. (You know who you are.) I'm grateful for all the support. My family members have been greatly supportive.

I also thank my Pastor Rev. James H. Reynolds, and my former Pastor, Rev. Franklin Gosnell, for bringing forth the word with boldness, and for being instrumental in my spiritual growth. Rev. John Smith, thank you for your support and counsel through the years, and for writing the Foreword for this book.

Special thanks to Margaret Edwards, also Marvin and Darlene Anthony, for staying by my side in bad times, as well as good times. Brenda Boone thanks for being so special in my life.

Thanks to Margaret Rhim for her constant encouragement. Janette Grant, thanks for entering my life, as I entered a new State. Lynn Stout, Myrna Shuman, Melvin and Mary Ward, thanks for being loyal long distance friends.

Carol Theresa Baker, Carolyn Davis, and Mary Keaton I'm blessed to have you in my life. I'm also blessed by everyone that reads this book. May you be blessed through the words on every page.

Dedication

This book is dedicated to my Lord and Savior, Jesus Christ.

All scripture is given by inspiration of God, and is profitable for doctrine, for reproof, for correction, for instruction in righteousness: (II Timothy 3:16)

In Loving Memory

Rev. John L. Toler
(April 1916 – December 1992)

Table of Contents

FOREWORD

Here is one of our newest writers on Devotional Readings and most inspiring poems, which are sensitive, wise and deeply rooted in the Word of God. These readings will provide nourishment for faith and daily encouragement for the Christian life. Here Barbara Caldwell speaks to our needs that are universal and in which all humanity shares. Their purpose is to focus the mind and the heart upon God as the Eternal Source and goal of life. Wherever they seem stumbling, weak and stammering, understanding that they are the utterance of one who sees through “a glass darkly.” What ever light they may bring at any point in another’s darkness is but a glimmer of “the Light that lighteth every human that cometh into the world.”

My personal thanks goes to my dear sojourner, Barbara Caldwell, who permitted me to have a share in this manuscript.

In those long midnight hours when the morning seems weeks away, the words of Barbara Caldwell have kept watch with me.

Rev. John H. Smith Sr. M. Div.
Union Baptist Church
Kenilworth, N. J.

How to Use This Book

Each poem has the correct day to be used, on the top right corner of each page. The scripture in chapter two coincide with the poetry in chapter one, they contain the same subject matter for each day. Chapter three contains thoughts for each day, they are based on the first two chapters. On page 96-97 you will find "How to Receive Jesus Christ as Your Lord and Savior."

This book can be used daily for spiritual encouragement and strength. All three chapters are to be read together. (Example: Read day #1, Chapter One, Two, and Three the same day.) Use this same system throughout the book. Chapter two and three are reasonably short, that you may easily digest the contents for each day.

Chapter 1

"Poetry"

Day #1

"My Friend"

My friend wakes me gently,
So that I can start my day.
He speaks to me softly,
As I walk along the way.

He tells me things to encourage me,
To nourish and cleanse my soul.
He walked the shores of Galilee,
Many years ago I'm told.

He healed the sick, he raised the dead,
He had mercy on sinners as
They pled.

He's the same yesterday, today,
And forever. I'll love him always,
And turn from him never.

At the close of the day,
He,ll hear me when I pray,
And forgive me of my sins each
And everyday.

Day #2

"The Realization of True Love"

Help me love my fellowman,
In every way I can.

Help me lend a helping hand,
To others in the land.

Help me see the beauty,
In another persons heart.
If I do I'll understand,
True love right from the start.

Help me not to be provoked,
By any evil word.

Help me to resist the urge,
As if I had not heard.

Faith, hope, and charity,
These three will always stand.
Charity will always be the greatest
Gift to man.

Day #3

"I Don't Know Where To Start Today"

I don't know where to start today, but Jesus
Will show me the way. There are many things
That I have to do, but I need guidance to
Carry them through.

Help me not to procrastinate, cause all my
Deadlines will surely be late. Help me know
My priorities, cause with this knowledge I
Can do things with ease.

Jesus is first on my list, each day
I'll never miss expressing my gratitude,
For such a day as this.

Day #4

"Guide Me"

Guide my eyes, that I might
See your beauty everyday.

Guide my mouth, that I might
Know what to say.

Guide my hands, that I might
Work to earn pay.

Guide my feet, as I walk
Along the way.

Guide my mind, to stay
Sane at all times.

Guide my soul, to be made whole,
Because you are in control.

Day #5

"Be Grateful"

Be grateful for the happy times,
Don't dwell on the sad.

Be grateful for the good times,
Don't worry about the bad.

Look forward to the future,
Don't look back on the past.

Don't worry about the present,
If things will be alright,
Or if they will last.

Just keep your eyes on Jesus,
Cause he won't let you down.

Don't worry about tomorrow,
Just be grateful for the here
And the now.

Day #6

"Life"

Life can make you happy.
Life can make you sad,
Many other times life can
Make you glad.

There will be ups and downs,
And things that make you frown.
Don't worry about a thing,
Cause you are heaven bound.

With Jesus you see, you can
Live life abundantly,
Because he died unselfishly
For you and me.

He died on the cross to set
Us free, from sin that could
Destroy us eternally.

Take no thought for your life,
Because Jesus will make
Everything right.

Continue to walk in the light,
And refuse to walk by sight.
Jesus will make your burdens light,
Just read his word day and night.

Day #7

"The Greatest Joy of All"

There are many things that cause joy,
But the joy that Jesus gives is everlasting.
No matter what circumstances come in our lives, whether good or bad, happy or sad.

We can always rejoice with unspeakable joy,
Full of glory as God's word tells the story.
As Christians we have much to be joyful about,
Our relationship with Christ,
Our invitation to Paradise.

Our daily walk with Jesus, should be a joy
In itself. The joy of the Lord is our strength,
And nothing else. Just keep your eyes on Jesus,
He won't let you down. In him you will be happy,
And joy will always abound.

Day #8

"Remember"

When your friends are gone,
When you don't hear sparrows
Chirping on the lawn.

Remember that God is near,
And you have nothing
To fear.

When burdens get you down,
And your head hangs down
Toward the ground.

Remember that God is always around,
And what a blessing in him
You've found.

When your bills are due,
And your dollars are few.

Remember that God loves you too,
He'll supply all your needs,
And carry you through.

Whatever state you're in,
Remember God is no respector
Of men. He'll always be your friend,
Just open your heart and let him in.

Day #9

"Help Us Realize"

Help us not to worry, help us
Not to fret. Help us realize,
That you haven't failed us yet.

Help us count our blessings,
When we're feeling down.
Help us
Realize that you'll always
Be around.

Help us climb the mountain,
When our trials appear.
Help us
Realize that we have nothing
To fear.

Help us stay encouraged,
When negatives start to flourish.
Help us realize, that your word
Will surely nourish.

Help us see a brighter day,
When darkness tends to loom.
Help us realize that
You're coming back soon.

Day #10

"Show Me The Way"

Show me the way dear Lord I pray.
I need your direction each and
Everyday.

You are the potter I am the clay.
Please mold me, and make me in
Your own special way.

Help me stay open to your guidance
Each day. As long as you lead me
I'll be O.K.

Thank you for the straight and
Narrow way. I'd rather walk that
Road than the broad anyday.

Day #11

"Anger"

Anger can happen quickly,
When you hold on to it,
It can make you sickly.

Anger can make you bitter,
It's worthless just
Like litter.

Anger happens to all of us,
When it's over it relieves disgust.

The fruits of the spirit can
Help us you know, to combat
Anger and give us a peaceful flow.

Day #12

"The Tongue"

The tongue can be a terrible thing
You see, it lives in the mouths of
You and me.

It can speak words of love sent from above,
Or it can cut like a knife when things
Don't go right.

It can gossip each day instead of pray,
It can utter a lie without delay.

Have you used this tongue today in a
Positive way? Have you used it wisely,
So you don't go astray?

Be controlled by the spirit each and
Everyday, and your tongue will be a
Blessing with every word you say.

Day #13

"Infallible"

There is one thing man is not,
and that is infallible. We try hard
as we can not to make a mistake,
But the chance of doing so is inevitable.
We disappoint each other. We do things
that are unexpected of us. There are
times that we surprise ourselves.
As Paul says "For that which I do
I allow not: for what I would,
that do I not; but what I hate,
that do I." No matter how hard we try,
We will never be infallible. The only
person that is truly infallible is
Jesus.

Day #14

"Jesus is the Way"

Jesus is the way, the truth and the life.
Some worship other gods,
But only Jesus can suffice.

He's the lily of the valley,
The bright and morning star.
When you surrender your life to him,
You'll find out who you really are.

He will give your life new meaning,
And direct your path each day.
If you put your trust in him,
You can make it come what may.

Day #15

"Never Ending Love"

My constant forever friend will love me
Till the end. When others let me down
He'll always be around.

He died to set me free, to trust him is
the key. Whatever the case may be he'll
Never forsake me.

Friends often come and go, some treat you
Like a foe. Disappointments make me feel
Low, then God's love hits me like an arrow
From a bow.

Day #16

"Strength"

Lord, give me strength to make
It through the day, please hold
My hand as I walk along the way.
Strength is made perfect in weakness,
Help me always to display meekness.

Strength is found in God's word,
Without it his voice cannot be heard.
The Lord is the strength of my life,
His peace and joy will always suffice.

Day #17

"While I Can"

Help me do all the good I can,
While I can, in every way I can.
We are here to minister to,
Not to be ministered to.
We should always ask the question,
"What would Jesus do?

Faith without works is dead,
What else is there to be said?
Continue to be spiritually led.
Read God's word and you'll surely
be fed.

Day #18

"Open Our Eyes"

Open our eyes that we may look to
The prize, the high calling in Christ
Jesus. We should never lay aside.

Open our eyes that we will always
Abide in the Lord who is our guide,
He will always walk by our side.

Open our eyes that we may empathize
With our brothers and sisters in Christ,
With whom we share our lives.

Open our eyes that we may realize
That if we think too high of ourselves
You can bring us down to size.

Open our eyes so that we will never
Compromise with the enemy who contrives
To destroy our very lives.

Day #19

"Incredible"

Do you think it's incredible
Jesus rose from the dead?
He rose on the third day just
Like he said.

Do you think it's incredible
How he calmed the raging sea,
For a group of disciples
Full of fear and disbelief?

Do you think it's incredible
How he turned water into wine?
This was quite easy, because he
Is the divine.

If you think these things are incredible
Just think of the inevitable,
He'll walk on the clouds, and
Carry us home in big crowds.

Day #20

"God's Handiwork"

The earth is the Lord's and he owns
All that dwell in it. You can see
His smile in the sun, his glory is easily
Seen in the firmament.

He displays his beauty in the flowers,
That he sprays with his own special scent.
Don't forget the trees, the birds, and the bees,
You can see God's art even in the leaves.

So next time you hear someone say
"Don't forget to smell the roses".
Just stop and look around,
Because God's handiwork truly abounds.

Day #21

"Lifted From the Darkness"

Lord, you lifted me from the darkness, and carried me into the light. The life I lived in the past
I know it wasn't right.

You showed me in a vision, you told me in your word, that if I'd give my life to you, you would save me
And give me sight.

Now my eyes are clear, I have nothing to fear.
You changed my life, and destroyed Satan's
device. To think of this is such a delight!

I'm happy to be free, oh look what you've done for
me. You lifted me out of the darkness and
Carried me into the light.

Day #22

"You Can't Depend on Man"

You can't depend on man, He'll hurt you if he can.
Sometimes you'll find someone loyal and true.
Sometimes others will make you disappointed and blue.

There is someone who will never let you down.
He'll never leave you, he'll always be around.
His name is Jesus he's loving and kind.
I can always depend on him, because he's truly a friend of mine.

Day #23

"A Friend"

A friend is one in whom you can
depend. In whom you can depend to
Give love and help you mend.

To help you mend from heartaches,
To help you mend from blues,
A friend will always encourage,
And often bring good news.

Good news to brighten your day,
To help you on your way. Loyal
Friends like this you need them
Everyday.

Secrets you can share, your plans
You can compare. To mistreat them
You'd never dare, to keep them is
Your prayer.

Day #24

"A Caregivers Prayer"

Give me patience and kindness, as I
Minister through the day. Open my ears
To be receptive, to everything you say.

Strengthen me mentally and physically,
To give my all and all. Help me to be
Available, when the person I care for calls.

Give me all the love I need, to be a
Successful caregiver indeed. Stay with
Me every hour, as I continue to
Help others through your power.

Day #25

"Faults"

I have faults, you have faults,
everybody has faults. We need to
deal with one anothers faults with
kindness, patience, and love

None of us are exempt from error,
we tend to look at our own faults,
rarer.

As 1st Corinthians 13 says by faith,
hope, and charity, we must be led.

With Jesus leading us, we can accept
much, but in our own strength we always
lose touch.

As time passes by from day to day our
faults will be fewer, because Jesus
heard us pray.

Day #26

"Friends and Enemies"

Friends and enemies, I pray blessings on
each today. Your friends will always
Love you, stand with you come what may.

Your enemies never like you, their aim is
To try and spite you.

Lord thank you for the friends you've put
In my life, it adds such a nice and
special spice.

I wish I didn't have these enemies, but
I'll continue to pray for them on my knees.

Day #27

"This Too Shall Pass"

The light bill is due, and the collecters are bugging you…this too shall pass.
Your friends are few, and your health is failing you…this too shall pass.
Your enemies are annoying you…this too shall pass.
You're unemployed, and your insurance is void…This too shall pass.
If all this is upsetting you…this too shall pass,
When we meet Jesus at last.

Day #28

"Impact"

Whet an impact you've made on
My life, because you are
Jesus Christ. You died to set
Me free, of sins whatever they
May be.

You made my life brand new.
Through your word, you told
Me nothing but truth.

Daily I read to hear you speak
To me. You're always there when
I call, whether I'm on my knees
Or standing tall.

I can communicate with you where
Ever I am, in my secret closet or
In the midst of man.

You've showered me with love from above.
I can picture the symbol of
A heavenly dove.

You're the only man who rose from
The dead, exactly the way he said.
One day I'll meet you face to face,
And forever experience your
Undying grace.

Day #29

"Success"

Success doesn't happen overnight,
keep working, and toiling till things
work out right.

Hard work will pay off, whatever the
cost. If you give up now, all will
surely be lost.

Keep trying, and trying till success
comes your way. You're closer to your
goal then you were yesterday.

Keep your eyes open, trust Jesus to
pave the way. He is the key to
success, we need him everyday.

Day #30

"The Day Is Done"

Through your help my accomplishments
Have been met. I've made it through
The day, and the moon is set.

Now as I lay down, sensing your spirit
All around. I tend to reflect on your
Goodness, and how you never let me down.

Another day is past, and my problems on
You I cast. I've learned to trust you
At last. With your help I can handle
Any task.

I don't have to worry about the events
Of the day, because God has taken care
Of it in his own special way.

This day is done, and regrets I have none,
Because I'm loved and guided by
God's only Son.

Chapter 2

"Scripture"

Day #1

"Jesus is Our Friend"

Greater love hath no man than this, that a man lay down his life for his friends.

Ye are my friends, if ye do whatsoever I command you.

Henceforth I call you not servants; for the servant knoweth not what his lord doeth: but I have called you friends; for all things that I have heard of my Father I have made known unto you.

John 15:13-15

Day #2

"What Is Love?"

Thou I speak with the tongues of men and of angels, and have not charity, I am become as a sounding brass, or a tinkling cymbal.

And thou I have the gift of prophecy, and understand all mysteries, and all knowledge; and thou I have all faith, so that I could remove mountains, and have not charity, I am nothing.

And thou I bestow all my goods to feed the poor, and though I give my body to be burned, and have not charity, it profiteth me nothing.

Charity suffereth long, and is kind; charity envieth not; charity vaunteth not itself, is not puffed up,

Doth not behave itself unseemly, seeketh not her own, is not easily provoked, thinketh no evil;

Rejoiceth not in iniquity, but rejoiceth in the truth;

Beareth all things, believeth all things, hopeth all things, endureth all things.

Charity never faileth: but whether there be prophecies, they shall fail; whether there be tongues, they shall cease; whether there be knowledge, it shall vanish away.

For we know in part, and we prophesy in part.

But when that which is perfect is come, then that which is in part shall be done away.

When I was a child, I spake as a child, I understood as a child I thought as a child: but when I became a man, I put away childish things.

For now we see through a glass, darkly; but then face to face: now I know in part; but then shall I know even as also I am known.

And now abideth faith, hope, charity, these three; but the greatest of these is charity.

I Corinthians 13

Day #3

"Priorities"

But seek ye first the kingdom of God, and his righteousness; and all these things shall be added unto you.

Matthew 6:33

Now it came to pass, as they went, that he entered into a certain village: and a certain woman named Martha received him into her house.

And she had a sister called Mary, which also sat at Jesus' feet, and heard his word.

But Martha was cumbered about much serving, and came to him, and said, "Lord, dost thou not care that my sister hath left me to serve alone? bid her therefore that she help me.

And Jesus answered and said unto her, Martha, Martha, thou art careful and troubled about many things:

But one thing is needful: and Mary hath chosen that good part, which shall not be taken away from her.

Luke 10:38-42

Day #4

"Open to God's Guidance"

For this God is our God for ever and ever: he will be our guide even unto death.

Psalm 48:14

Order my steps in thy word: and let not any iniquity have dominion over me.

Psalm 119:133

Teach me to do thy will; for thou art my God: thy spirit is good; lead me into the land of uprightness.

Psalm 143:10

Therefore turn thou to thy God: keep mercy and judgment, and wait on thy God continually.

Hosea 12:6

Day #5

"Be Thankful"

It is a good thing to give thanks unto the Lord, and to sing praises unto thy name, O most High:

Psalm 92:1

Enter into his gates with thanksgiving, and into his courts with praise: be thankful unto him, and bless his name.

Psalm 100:4

O give thanks unto the Lord, for he is good: for his mercy endureth for ever.

Psalm 107:1

In everything give thanks: for this is the will of God in Christ Jesus concerning you.

I Thessalonians 5:18

Day #6

"Life"

Man that is born of a woman is of few days, and full of trouble.

Job 14:1

To everything there is a season, and a time to every purpose under the heaven:

Ecclesiastes 3:1

For I reckon that the sufferings of this present time are not worthy to be compared with the glory that shall be revealed in us.

Romans 8:18

Day #7

"Joy"

…neither be ye sorry; for the joy of the Lord is your strength.

Nehemiah 8:10 b

These things have I spoken unto you, that my joy might remain in you, and that your joy might be full.

John 15:11

Whom having not seen, ye love; in whom, though now ye see him not, yet believing, ye rejoice with joy unspeakable and full of glory:

I Peter 1:8

Day #8

"You Are Not Alone"

Fear thou not; for I am with thee: be not dismayed; for I am thy God: I will strengthen thee; yea, I will help thee; yea, I will uphold thee with the right hand of my righteousness.

Isaiah 41:10

Go ye therefore, and teach all nations, baptizing them in the name of the Father, and of the Son, and of the Holy Ghost:

Teaching them to observe all things whatsoever I have commanded you: and, lo, I am with you, alway, even unto the end of the world. Amen.

Matthew 28:19-20

Let your conversation be without covetousness; and be content with such things as ye have: for he hath said, I will never leave thee, nor forsake thee.

Hebrews 13:5

Day #9

"Realizing the Power of God"

God is my strength and power: and he maketh my way perfect.

II Samuel 22:33

Forasmuch as there is none like unto thee, O Lord; thou art great, and thy name is great in might.

Jeremiah 10:6

Let every soul be subject unto the higher powers. For there is no power but of God: the powers that be are ordained of God.

Romans 13:1

Day #10

"Leaning on Jesus"

Thou wilt shew me the path of life: in thy presence is fulness of joy; at thy right hand there are pleasures for evermore.

Psalm 16:11

Shew me thy ways, O Lord; teach me thy paths.

Lead me in thy truth, and teach me: for thou art the God of my salvation; on thee do I wait all the day.

Psalm 25:4-5

Day #11

"Beware of Anger"

He that is soon angry dealeth foolishly: and a man of wicked devices is hated.

Proverbs 14:17

A soft answer turneth away wrath: but grievous words stir up anger.

Proverbs 15:1

Be not hasty in thy spirit to be angry: for anger resteth in the bosom of fools.

Ecclesiastes 7:9

Be ye angry, and sin not: let not the sun go down upon your wrath:

Ephesians 4:26

Day #12

"The Tongue"

Whoso keepeth his mouth and his tongue keepeth his soul from troubles.

Proverbs 21:23

And whatever you do in word or deed, do all in the name of the Lord Jesus, giving thanks to God and the Father by him.

Colossians 3:17

If any man among you seem to be religious, and bridleth not his tongue, but deceiveth his own heart, this man's religion is vain.

James 1:26

For in many things we offend all. If any man offend not in word, the same is a perfect man, and able also to bridle the whole body.

James 3:2

Day #13

"Realizing How Imperfect We Are"

Oh God, thou knowest my foolishness; and my sins are not hid from thee.

Psalm 69:5

For there is not a just man upon earth, that doeth good and sinneth not.

Ecclesiastes 7:20

But we are all as an unclean thing, and all our righteousness are as filthy rags; and we all do fade as a leaf; and our iniquities, like the wind, have taken us away.

Isaiah 64:6

Day #14

"The Only Way"

And Jesus said unto them, I am the bread of life: he that cometh to me shall never hunger; and he that believeth on me shall never thirst.

John 6:35

Jesus saith unto him, I am the way, the truth, and the life: no man cometh unto the Father, but by me.

John 14:6

For there is one God, and one mediator between God and men, the man Christ Jesus;

I Timothy 2:5

Day #15

"Who Will Always Love Us?"

For God so loved the world, that he gave his only begotten Son, that whosoever believeth in him should not perish, but have everlasting life.

John 3:16

But God commendeth his love toward us, in that, while we were yet sinners, Christ died for us.

Romans 5:8

And we have known and believed the love that God hath to us. God is love; and he that dwelleth in love dwelleth in God, and God in him.

I John 4:16

Day #16

"Where is Our Strength Found?"

I will love thee, O Lord, my strength.

The Lord is my rock, and my fortress, and my deliverer; my God, my strength, in whom I will trust; my buckler, and the horn of my salvation, and my high tower.

Psalm 18:1-2

God is our refuge and strength, a very present help in trouble.

Psalm 46:1

Sing aloud unto God our strength: make a joyful noise unto the God of Jacob.

Psalm 81:1

Behold, God is my salvation; I will trust, and not be afraid: for the Lord JEHOVAH is my strength and my song; he also is become my salvation.

Isaiah 12:2

Day #17

"Do What You Can While You Can"

Let your light so shine before men, that they may see your good works, and glorify your Father which is in heaven.

Matthew 5:16

I must work the works of him that sent me, while it is day: the night cometh, when no man can work.

John 9:4

Therefore, my beloved brethren, be ye stedfast, unmoveable, always abounding in the work of the Lord, forasmuch as ye know that your labour is not vain in the Lord.

I Corinthians 15:58

Day #18

"Help Us See Clearly"

Hatred stirreth up strifes: but love covereth all sins.
Proverbs 10:12

Better is little with the fear of the Lord than great treasure and trouble therewith.
Proverbs 15:16

And thou shalt love the Lord thy God with all thy heart, and with all thy soul, and with all thy mind, and with all thy strength: this is the first commandment.

And the second is like, namely this, Thou shalt love thy neighbour as thyself. There is none other commandment greater than these.
Mark 12:30-31

And he said unto them, Take heed, and beware of covetousness: for a man's life consisteth not in the abundance of the things which he possesseth.
Luke 12:15

If ye abide in me, and my words abide in you, ye shall ask what he will, and it shall be done unto you.
John 15:7

Day #19

"The Awesomeness of Jesus"

But the men marvelled, saying, What manner of man is this, that even the winds and the sea obey him!

Matthew 8:27

For with God nothing shall be impossible.

Luke 1:37

For the Lord himself shall descend from heaven with a shout, with the voice of the archangel, and with the trump of God: and the dead in Christ shall rise first: Then we which are alive and remain shall be caught up together with them in the clouds, to meet the Lord in the air: and so shall we ever be with the Lord.

I Thessalonians 4:16-17

Day #20

"The Hand of God"

Thou hast set all the borders of the earth: thou hast made summer and winter.

Psalm 74:17

I remember the days of old; I meditate on all thy works; I muse on the work of thy hands.

Psalm 143:5

He hath made the earth by his power, he hath established the world by his wisdom, and hath stretched out the heavens by his discretion.

Jeremiah 10:12

Day #21

"A Changed Life"

Therefore if any man be in Christ, he is a new creature: old things are passed away; behold, all things are become new.

II Corinthians 5:17

Mortify therefore your members which are upon the earth; fornication, uncleanness, inordinate affection, evil concupiscence, and covetousness, with is idolatry:

But now ye also put off all these; anger wrath, malice, blasphemy, filthy communication out of your mouth.

Lie not one to another, seeing that ye have put off the old man with his deeds;

And have put on the new man, which is renewed in knowledge after the image of him that created him:

Colossians 3:5, 8-10

Day #22

"Trust In God, Not In Man"

Behold, in this thou art not just: I will answer thee, that God is greater than man.

Job 33:12

It is better to trust in the Lord than to put confidence in man.

Psalm 118:8

God is faithful, by whom ye were called unto the fellowship of his Son Jesus Christ our Lord.

I Corinthians 1:9

Day #23

"How to be a Friend"

And it came to pass, when he had made an end of speaking unto Saul, that the soul of Jonathan was knit with the soul of David, and Jonathan loved him as his own soul.

I Samuel 18:1

A friend loveth at all times…

Proverbs 17:17a

A man that hath friends must shew himself friendly: and there is a friend that sticketh closer than a brother.

Proverbs 18:24

Day #24

"The Character of a Caregiver"

But a certain Samaritan, as he journeyed, came where he was: and when he saw him, he had compassion on him,

Luke 10:33

Do all things without murmurings and disputings:

Philippians 2:14

Finally be ye all of one mind, having compassion one of another, love as brethren, be pitiful, be courteous:

I Peter 3:8

Day #25

"We All Have Faults"

Who can say, I have made my heart clean, I am pure from my sin?

Proverbs 20:9

Judge not, that ye be not judged.

Matthew 7:1

Thou hypocrite, first cast out the beam out of thine own eye; and then shalt thou see clearly to cast out the mote out of thy brother's eye.

Matthew 7:5

Day #26

"Bless Our Enemies, As Well As Our Friends"

If thine enemy be hungry, give him bread to eat; and if he be thirsty, give him water to drink:

For thou shalt heap coals of fire upon his head, and the Lord shall reward thee.

Proverbs 25:21-22

But I say unto you, Love your enemies, bless them that curse you, do good to them that hate you, and pray for them which despitefully use you, and persecute you;

Matthew 5:44

Bless them which persecute you: bless, and curse not.

Romans 12:14

Day #27

"A Better Day is Coming"

For I reckon that the sufferings of this present time are not worthy to be compared with the glory which shall be revealed in us.

Romans 8:18

For God hath not appointed us to wrath, but to obtain salvation by our Lord Jesus Christ,
Who died for us, that, whether we wake or sleep, we should live together with him.

I Thessalonians 5:9-10

And God shall wipe away all tears from their eyes; and there shall be no more death, neither sorrow, nor crying, neither shall there be any more pain: for the former things are passed away.

Revelation 21:4

Day #28

"What An Impact Jesus Can Make"

I will bless the Lord at all times: his praise shall continually be in my mouth.

Psalm 34:1

For the Lord is a great God, and a great King above all gods.

Psalm 95:3

For the Lord is great, and greatly to be praised: he is to be feared above all gods.

Psalm 96:4

Remember his marvellous works that he hath done; his wonders, and the judgments of his mouth;

Psalm 105:5

Day #29

"How to Succeed"

This book of the law shall not depart out of thy mouth; but thou shalt meditate therein day and night, that thou mayest observe to do according to all that is therein: for then thou shalt make thy way prosperous, and then thou shalt have good success.

Joshua 1:8

Blessed is the man that walketh not in the counsel of the ungodly, nor standeth in the way of sinners, nor sitteth in the seat of the scornful.

But his delight is in the law of the Lord; and in his law doth he meditate day and night.

And he shall be like a tree planted by the rivers of water, that bringeth forth his fruit in his season; his leaf also shall not wither, and whatsoever he doeth shall prosper.

Psalm 1:1-3

Day #30

"The End of the Day"

I laid me down and slept; I awaked; for the Lord sustained me.

Psalm 3:5

Stand in awe, and sin not; commune with your own heart upon your bed, and be still. Selah.

Psalm 4:4

My soul shall be satisfied as with marrow and fatness; and my mouth shall praise thee with joyful lips:

When I remember thee upon my bed, and meditate on thee in the night watches.

Psalm 63:5-6

Chapter 3

"Thoughts for Each Day"

Thought #1

Jesus will always be our friend. The only way we can truly be his friend, is to keep his commandments. We will never find another friend like Jesus. It is comforting to know that we can call on him 24 hours a day, and never have to deal with a busy signal, or an answering machine. We can cast all our cares on him, because he cares for us. He can always be trusted with our secrets, and concerns. There is no other friend like him!

Thought #2

If we say we love God and hate our brother, we are a liar. When we love others their faults can be dealt with prayerfully. Proverbs 10:12 lets us know "Hatred stirreth up strifes: but love covereth all sins.

The real test of love is to love the unlovable. It is easy to love those who love us, but what about those who don't? Love should be expressed in deed, and not words only. Actions always speak louder than words.

Thought #3

Keep your priorities in order! Jesus should always be first on our list. The days activities are accomplished much better, when we start the day with Jesus. Prayer, Bible Study, and Biblical Meditation are more beneficial than any cup of coffee!

Thought #4

The Holy Bible is our road map through life. As we study the scriptures God guides us in every area of our lives. Jesus sent the Holy Spirit to guide us. Being led by the Holy Spirit assures us that we're on the right path.

Thought #5

Just to wake up in the morning is a blessing from God. There is so much to be grateful for. Nothing should be taken for granted. Always remember every good, and perfect gift comes from God. Never neglect letting God know how grateful you are for his bountiful blessings.

Thought #6

Life holds many surprises, we never know what's ahead from day to day. When we allow God to control our lives he gives us strength to deal with any situation. Living your life as a Christian is the most rewarding experience a person can have. Jesus promised that he came to give us life, and life more abundantly.

Thought #7

To be joyful is to be intensely happy. Many incidents that we've experienced only bring a temporary joy. The joy that Jesus gives is everlasting. No matter what situation we're going through with Jesus in our lives joy is always present. The joy of the Lord is our strength!

Thought #8

Take a moment to think about the faithfulness of God. Has he ever let you down? From our mother's womb, all the way up until the present time God has done many wonderful things in our lives. We must not forget all his benefits. He will never leave us alone, he's only a prayer away.

Thought #9

Sometimes we don't realize the wonderful working power of God. We must ask ourselves from time to time. Who woke us up this morning? Who started us on our way? Who can we look to for our every need? Eventhough we know the answer to these questions, we quickly realize Jesus is our all in all.

Thought #10

If you ask the Lord to direct you he will. We can do nothing in our own strength. Proverbs 3:5-6 states "Trust in the Lord with all thine heart; and lean not unto thine own understanding." "In all thy ways acknowledge him, and he shall direct thy paths."

Thought #11

The enemy works hard at sending someone to make us angry. Jesus is the only one who can truly curb anger. Sin is present when we hold on to anger that leads to a path of bitterness. Colossians 3:8 states that we should "put off anger", and Ephesians 4:26 states "Be angry, and sin not: let not the sun go down upon your wrath."

Thought #12

The tongue should be used to build up others, and not tear them down. Our tongue should be used to give a blessing, and not a curse. Think of all the positive things we can say with our tongue. Refuse the negative, and practice the positive. "Not that which goeth into the mouth defileth a man; but that which cometh out of the mouth, this defileth a man." (Matthew 15:11)

Thought #13

Only Jesus is infallible. None of us are free from error. We don't have to live our lives, trying to be perfectionist. Jesus is always around to strengthen our weakness, forgive our mistakes, and help us to avoid repeating the same mistakes. If we were perfect we wouldn't need Jesus.

Thought #14

There is only one way to God, and that is through Jesus. Beware of false religions who focus on leading you to a road of destruction. We are living in the last days, and there will be many cults springing up throughout the world. I John 4:1 states “Beloved, believe not every spirit, but try the spirits whether they are of God: because many false prophets are gone into the world. Keep your spiritual eyes open!

Thought #15

All friends are not forever friends, but Jesus is. He will be with us in good times, bad times, and at all times. Jesus loves us, he'll never turn against us, as men sometimes do. Thank God for his son Jesus!

Thought #16

Day by day we are strengthened by the power of God, and his word. Sometimes we are not aware of our growth until we look back on a situation that happened in the past, and realize we handle it better now than ever before. There is nothing we can do to strengthen our spiritual lives except totally surrender everything to Jesus. He can handle everything, we can handle nothing ourselves. Only Jesus can make us stronger.

Thought #17

Life is really short according to God's timing. While we are on earth, we should do all we can to help our fellowman. When we do good to others, we are actually doing it to Jesus. For example when we visit the sick, feed the hungry, clothe the naked, Jesus said, "as ye have done it unto the least of these my brethren, you have done it unto me." (Matthew 25:35-40)

Thought #18

If you lack wisdom ask of God, who gives to all men liberally, and upbraideth not; and it shall be given to you. (James 1:5.) Ask God to let you see his word, and his way clearly.

Before you study your Bible, pray "Open thou mine eyes, that I may behold wondrous things out of thy law." This is found in (Psalm 119:18.) This scripture will help you to understand God's word, and how to apply it to your life.

Thought #19

Who else could walk on water, or calm the raging sea? Jesus brought healing, holiness, and hope to the wounded and broken hearted. He made eternal life available to everyone. Satan is powerful, but Jesus is all powerful. He is awesome!

Thought #20

If we look for it, we can see God's hand at work in many things that surround us. When you look at the sky, the flowers, birds and bees, God's work can easily be seen. Look at us, our birth is remarkable. Psalm 139:14 states, "I will praise thee; for I am fearfully and wonderfully made: marvelous are thy works, and that my soul knoweth right well." Take a look around, God's handiwork can always be found. Begin with yourself, there is no one exactly like you.

Thought #21

For all have sinned, and come short of the glory of God; see (Romans 3:23). None of us were born free from sin, we've all sinned and made mistakes that we are not proud of.

Jesus is able to cleanse us, and make us new. "Come now, and let us reason together saith the Lord: though your sins be as scarlet, they shall be as white as snow; though they be red like crimson, they shall be as wool." (Isaiah 1:18)

Thought #22

Man will sometimes disappoint you, but you can always depend on Jesus. No matter what we're going through Jesus will come to our aid. Don't be discouraged when others let you down, Jesus will always be around.

Thought #23

Friends should be loving, caring, forgiving, and loyal. When a friend is loyal, they will never hurt or disappoint you. A friend will always be true until the end. To have one friend of this caliber, is truly a blessing from God.

Thought #24

Sickness can overtake us at anytime, we must keep this in mind. Caring for others, who can't fully take care of themselves, should be a pleasure. We may tire in a long-term situation, but we must depend on Jesus to give us strength.

Do unto others, as we would have them do unto us. The kindness that we give to others, will always be returned to us in someway. This is the same concept as "you reap what you sow."

Thought #25

Do you know anyone that doesn't have faults? Life would be so much better, if we would stop finding fault in one another. If we ask God to correct our faults, we would find it easier to deal with the faults of others. The bottom line is we all have faults.

Thought #26

No weapon formed against thee shall prosper…(Isaiah 54:17a.) It is stated in (Proverbs 16:7) "When a man's ways please the Lord, he maketh even his enemies to be at peace with him." With Jesus on our side, we don't have to worry about our enemies, just love them and pray for them.

Thought #27

When we all get to heaven, what a day of rejoicing that will be. Our problems will be over, when we reach our heavenly home. We won't have to worry about anything. Heartaches and pains will be over. Praise God!

Thought #28

You will walk different, talk different, and live different, if Jesus has truly made an impact on your life. The way we live our daily lives, is a testimony to the impact that Jesus has made on us. Are you a living testimony today?

Thought #29

Without Jesus we can't truly succeed in anything. If we always put Jesus first, obey him, and seek his will we can't go wrong. Jesus is the answer to success, not education, not money, not anything else.

Thought #30

The end of the day is a perfect time, to reflect on the move of God throughout your day. Our last thoughts before falling asleep, should be about Jesus. Don't worry about tomorrow, it will take care of itself. God has the next day in his control.

How to Receive Jesus Christ as Your Lord and Savior

That if thou shalt confess with thy mouth the Lord Jesus, and shalt believe in thine heart that God hath raised him from the dead, thou shalt be saved.

For with the heart man believeth unto righteousness; and with the mouth confession is made unto salvation.

Romans 10:9-10

Four Steps to Receive Christ

1. ADMIT – That you are a sinner.
2. REPENT – Turn away from your sins.
3. BELIEVE – Jesus died on the cross for your sins, rose on the third day, and that he is truly the Son of God.
4. RECEIVE – Ask Jesus into your heart and life through prayer.

Pray the following prayer, or one similar.

Dear Lord Jesus:

I admit that I'm a sinner. I believe you died on the cross for my sins, rose on the third day, and that you are truly the Son of God. I now turn away from my sins. Lord, forgive me, cleanse me, and make me new. Please come into my heart and life. Thank you for saving me.

Amen

Now that you've received Christ:

1. Read your Bible daily.
2. Pray everyday.
3. Find a Church as soon as possible.
4. Share your faith in Christ, by witnessing and testifying.